Contents

- **2** Introduction/The Romans
- **4** York 71 CE
- **6** York 150 CE
- **8** York 208 CE
- **10** York 306 CE
- **12** The Legionary Fortress 150 CE
- **14** The Legionary Fortress 300 CE
- **16** The Colonia
- **18** The Multangular Tower
- **20** Bootham Bar
- **22** The Fortress Bathhouse
- **24** The Principia
- **26** The Barracks
- **28** The Granaries
- **30** The Ninth Legion
- **32** Roman York today

Symbols used in this guide

- **1** Roman site, with visible remains[1]
- **2** Roman site, with no visible remains[1]
- **3** Speculative location of Roman site (Other Roman towns of York's importance had these sites, but no evidence of them has been found in York)
- — Roman wall, no visible remains[2]
- — Post-Roman wall, with visible remains

- Extent of Roman York
- **A** The Yorkshire Museum
- **B** Undercroft Museum, York Minster
- **C** Roman Bath Museum

1. Some of the reconstructions are speculative, but are based on similar versions found in Roman Britain.

2. The city wall, south of the River Ouse may follow the line of a Roman Wall, but no evidence has yet been found.

Roman York looking north, 300 CE.

Introduction

The area where York is located was occupied for around five centuries before the Roman invasion. This was the territory of the *Brigantes*, a powerful and warlike tribe who for many years after the invasion proved difficult to control.

The Roman occupation and growth of the city is the focus of this guide, exploring the period from 70 CE to 306 CE. After this date the Roman Empire started a gradual decline and by 410 CE Britain was under constant attack by marauding Anglo-Saxons.

The guide brings to life how York **could** have looked, with full-colour images all looking north *(unless specified otherwise)* and detailed maps showing where each site is in present-day York.

Towns and cities
The Romans defined towns and cities differently to how we do in the present day. They had three main types of town:
- *A Colonia, which was a rough equivalent of a city.*
- *A Municipium, which was slightly less important than a colonia.*
- *A Civitas capital, which was a broad equivalent of a large market town.*

The Romans called pre-Roman towns 'oppida'.

The Romans

The city of Rome in central Italy was formed around 800 BCE and grew over the centuries into the Roman Empire, which covered most of Europe, the Middle East and North Africa. It was a highly sophisticated and technologically advanced society, with a huge army, major roads and large cities. Britain at that time was a mysterious place with fierce tribes and valuable metals, which became the focus of attempted invasions in 55 BCE and 54 BCE by *Julius Caesar*.
Those invasions were repelled by local tribes and the Romans did not try again to invade Britain for almost 100 years.
By 43 CE the *Emperor Claudius (who needed the army's support)* decided to invade Britain, focusing his initial attack on the east of England. By 70 CE Roman forces were moving to occupy the area where York now stands...

Visiting York
York lies about 211 miles north of London.
There are three main museums which show Roman York in depth: the Yorkshire Museum, York Minster's Undercroft Museum and the Roman Bath Museum. Remains of the Roman city wall and partial remains of other Roman sites can also be seen around the city.

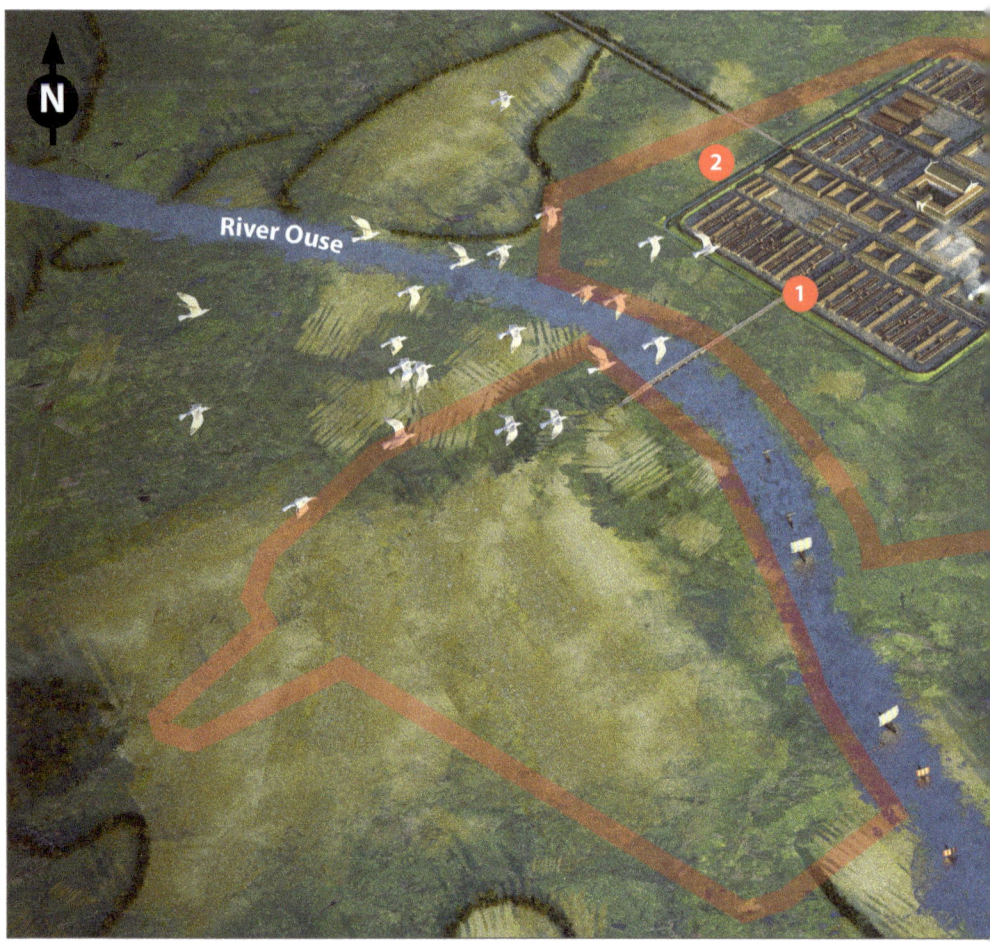

A view of York, looking north, 71 CE.

York 71 CE

Before the Roman invasion York was part of the territory of the *Brigantes*, ruled from a huge hill-fort 50 miles *(80 km)* north of York at Stanwick. They had settled in the area during the Iron Age and were fiercely protective of their territory. As the Romans moved into the area they chose the area where the River Ouse meets the River Foss.

The Romans possibly built a temporary *Castra (camp)* as they were fighting the *Brigantes*. This would have had tents, ditches and *Sudes (stakes)* wall defences, which could be prepared rapidly each night. Nothing was sited too close to the perimeter defences, to stay out of range of enemy thrown weapons such as spears. The Romans met strong resistance. After pitched battles the *Brigantes* continued to attack the Romans until around 71 CE when a permanent Roman fortress was established. This was easy to defend and supply, being next to the two rivers.

Key

— *Extent of Roman York*
1. *Roman Fortress (Note some of the buildings and roads under construction)*
2. *Wooden walls*

Contains Ordnance Survey data © Crown copyright and database right 2025

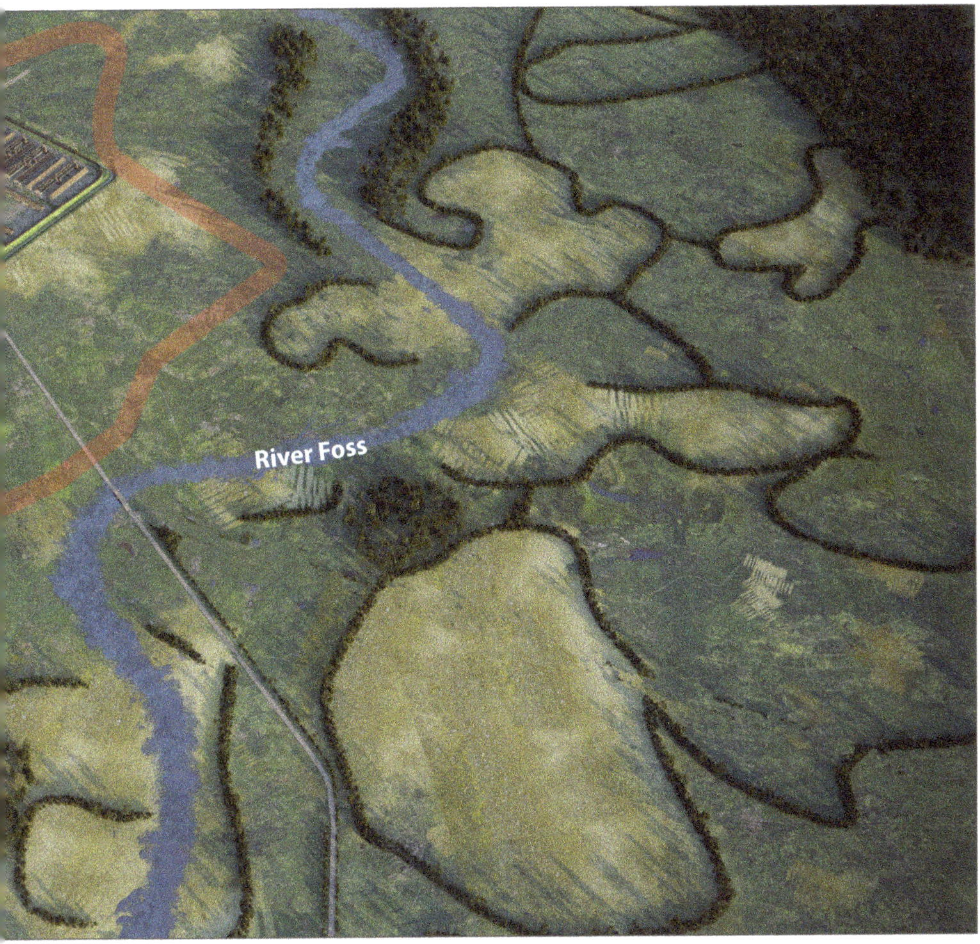

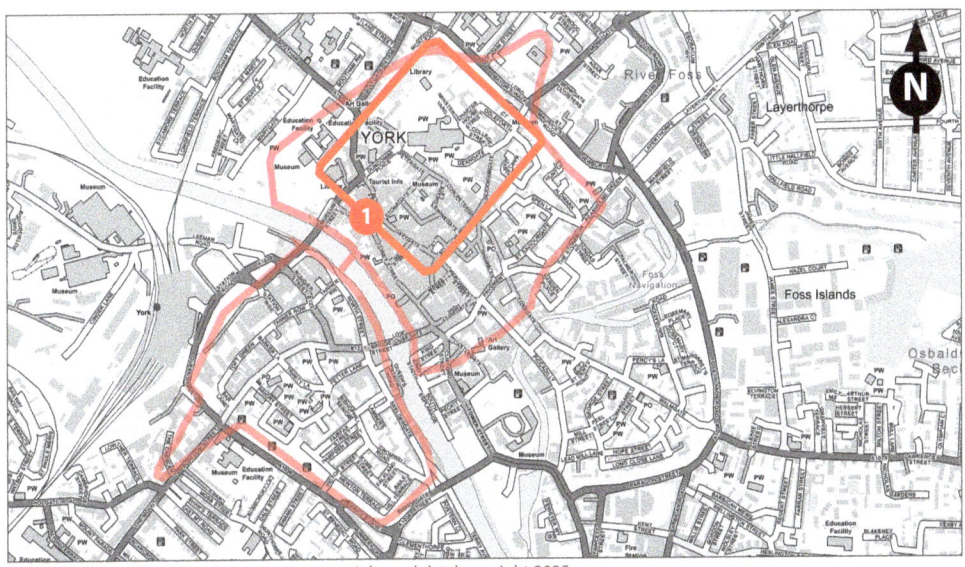

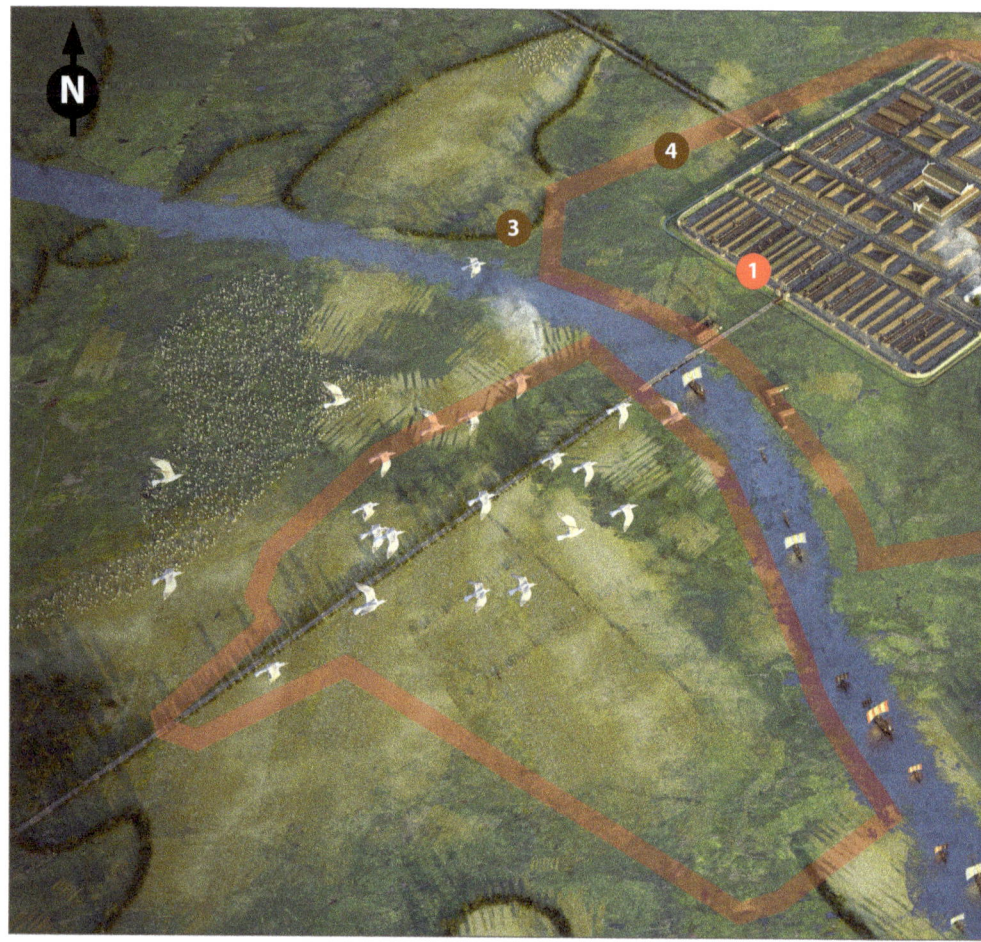

A view of York, looking north, 150 CE.

York 150 CE

Around 71 CE a permanent fortress was established by the *Legio IX Hispana (Ninth Spanish Legion)* and would have housed over 5000 men. The fortress was named *Eboracum* (adapting the local Celtic name Eboracon, which may have meant 'The place of the Boar'). Around 119 CE the *Legio VI Victrix (Victorious Sixth Legion)* replaced the depleted Ninth Spanish Legion. Part of their duties included building *Hadrian's Wall*[1] (about 130 miles/209km north of York) and upgrading the fortress's defences with stone walls and towers. *If* the fortress followed a similar pattern to Chester and Caerleon in Wales, by this time it would have had an amphitheatre, although no evidence has yet been found. Outside the fortress a large settlement called a *Canaba (equivalent to a village)* was growing, which housed shops and other facilities to cater for the fortress's needs.

1. Built by Emperor Hadrian to defend against northern tribes.

Key

- Extent of Roman York
- 1 Roman Fortress
- 2 Canaba
- 3 Possible Amphitheatre
- 4 Possible Annexe

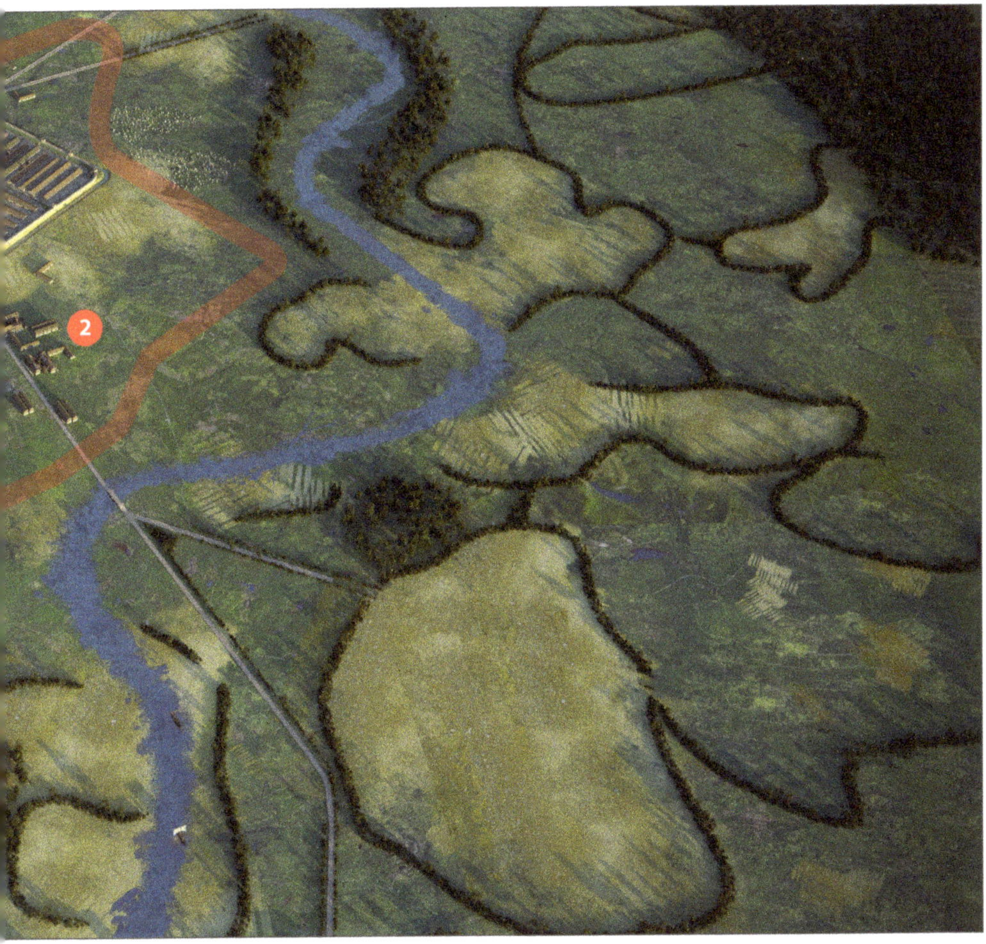

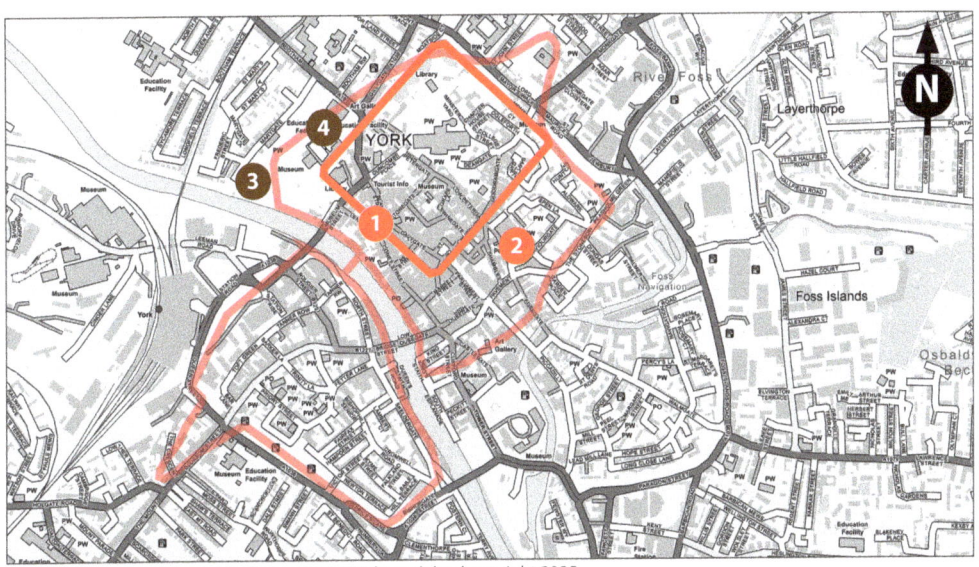

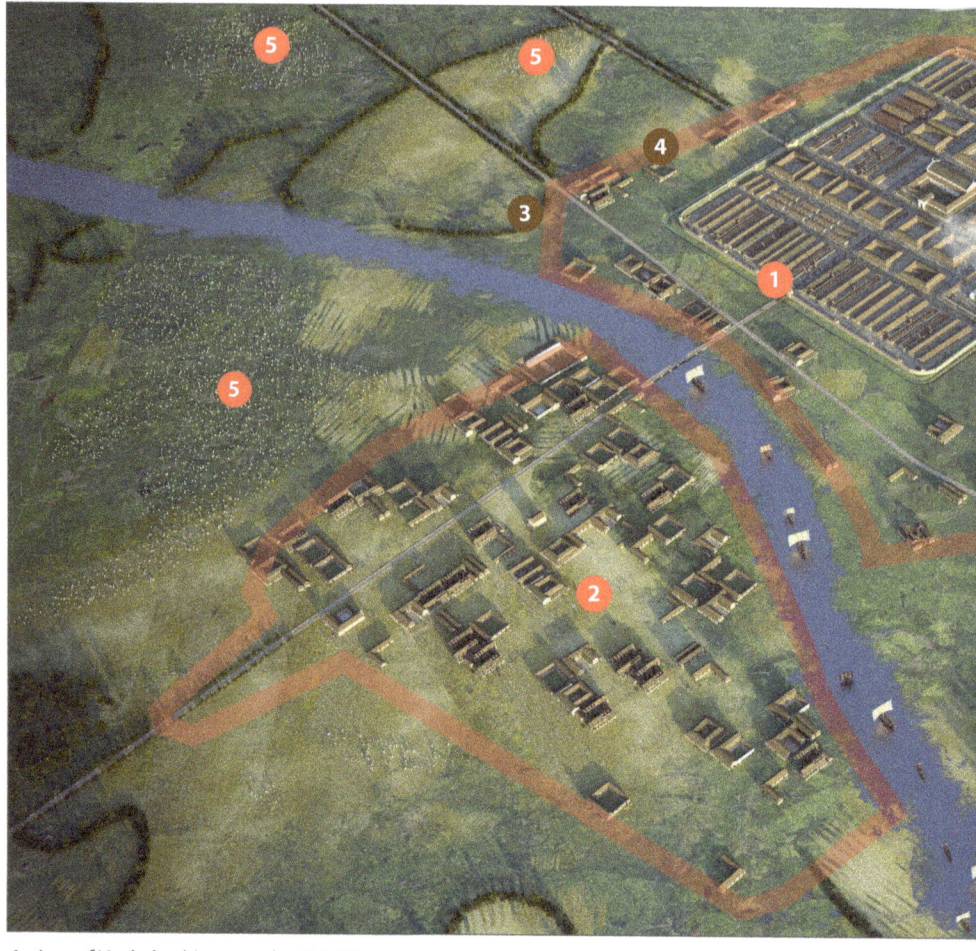

A view of York, looking north, 208 CE.

York 208 CE

By this time the Roman Empire was gradually starting to crumble. *Dio Cassius (a Roman historian)* commented that the empire went *from a kingdom of gold to one of rust and iron*. As part of this upheaval the *Emperor Septimius Severus* actually ruled the whole empire for a few years from York while fighting the northern tribes. At that time Britain was split into two areas: *Britannia Superior (south)* and *Britannia Inferior (north)* with York *(Eboracum)* governing the north. The Emperor *(born in Libya)* brought with him his wife *Julia Domna (born in Syria),* who was well respected for her political influence. He also brought over 35,000 troops and his two sons. But the military campaigns in *Caledonia (northern Scotland)* took their toll and the Emperor died of illness in York around 211 CE. He was succeeded by his sons, who quickly started to fight amongst themselves, against his wishes.

Key
- Extent of Roman York
- 1 Roman Fortress
- 2 Canabae
- 3 Possible Amphitheatre
- 4 Possible Annexe
- 5 Cemetery

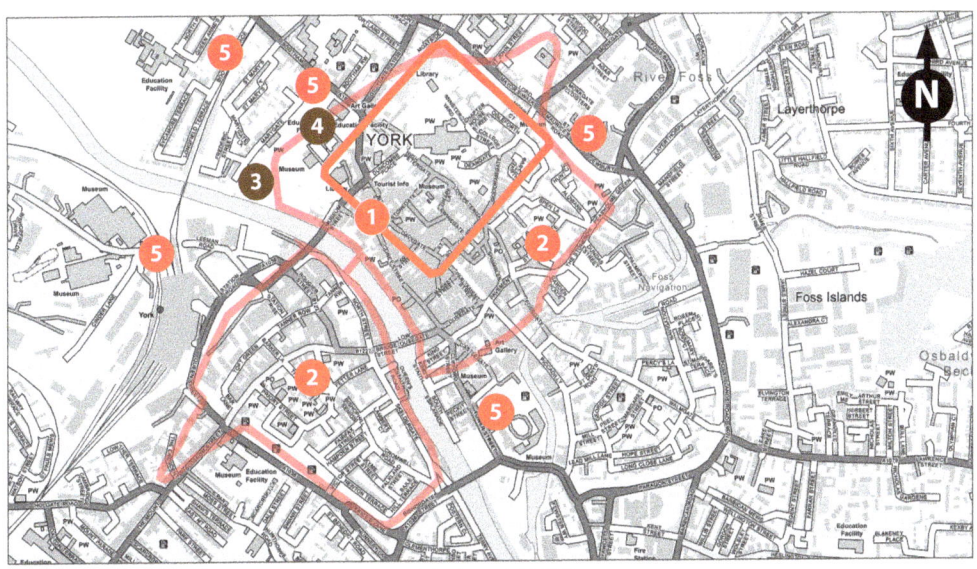

A view of York, looking north, 306 CE.

York 306 CE

In the midst of political intrigue and upheaval *Constantine* travelled to Britain to join his father *Emperor Constantius Chlorus (who ruled the western part of the Roman Empire)*. The Emperor *(and his forces)* were fighting against the *Picts (tribes from present day Scotland)*. Unfortunately the Emperor died in the summer of 306 CE. As he died he made his son *Constantine* the new emperor. This took place in York with the approval of the Roman Legions. He then proceeded to strengthen the empire helping bring reforms, which led to him being known as *Constantine the Great*. Remains have been found of many public buildings, including a public Bathhouse and a temple dedicated to *Serapis*[1].

1. Serapis was a Greek/Egyptian god who was worshipped by some Romans, including Emperor Severus. The main image includes speculative views of how the Temple of Serapis and the Public Bathhouse may have looked.

Key

- Extent of Roman York
- **1** Road to Catterick
- **2** Road to Malton
- **3** Road to Stamford Bridge
- **4** Road to Brough
- **5** Road to Lincoln
- **6** Road to Tadcaster
- **7** Fortress
- **8** Colonia
- **9** Possible Amphitheatre
- **10** Possible Annexe
- **11** Public Bathhouse
- **12** Temple of Serapis
- **13** Possible Colonia Wall

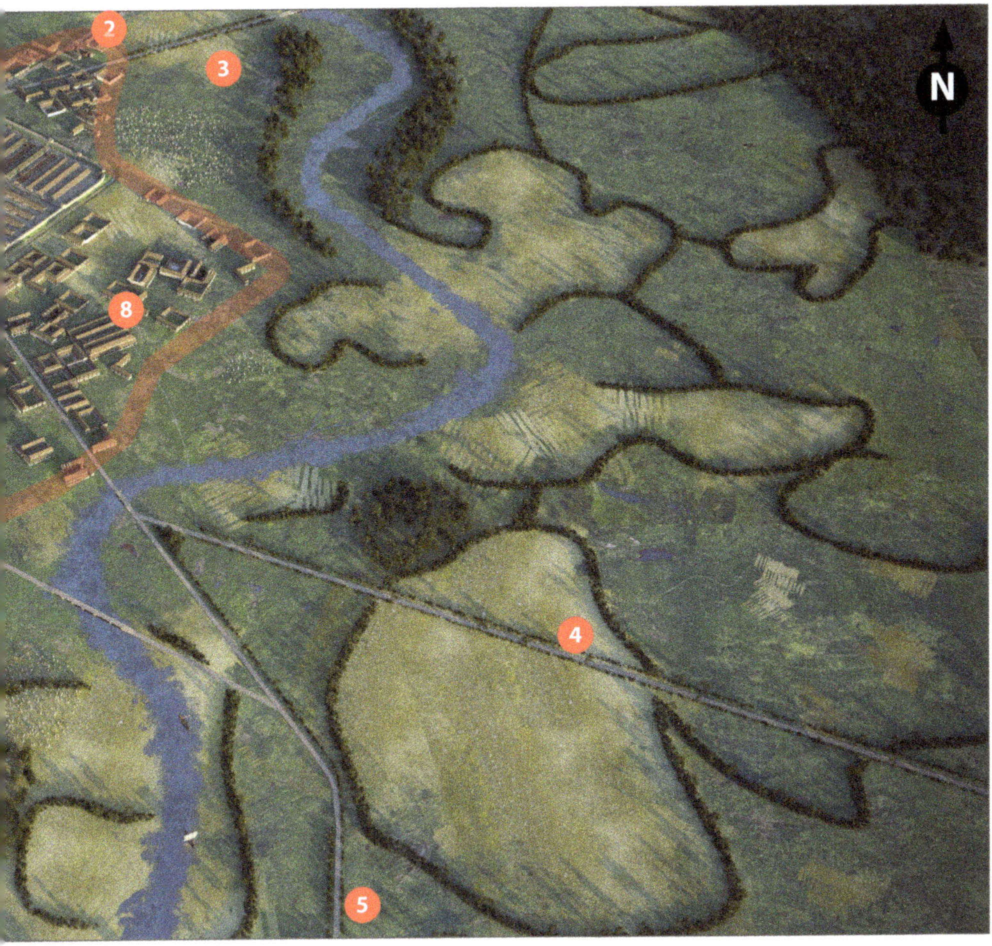

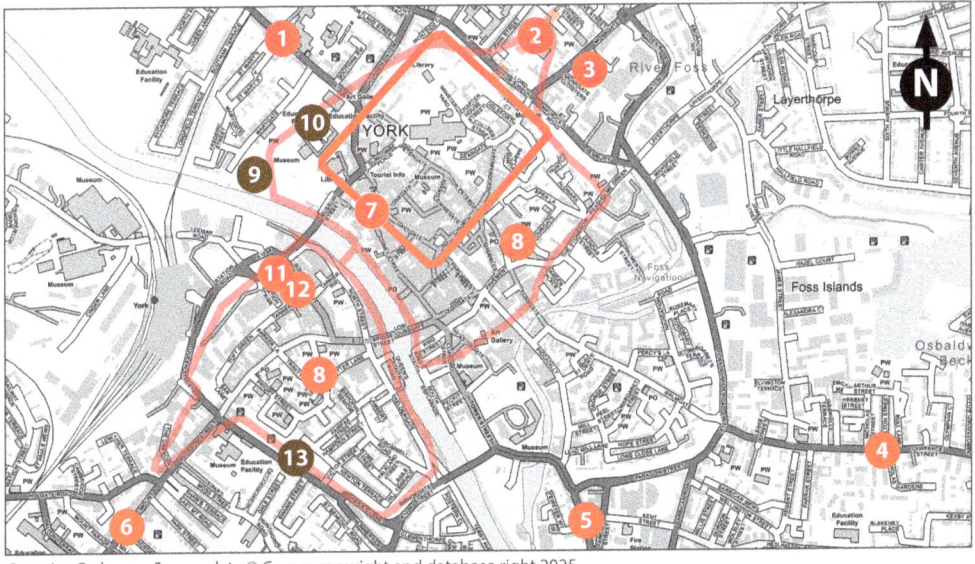

12. The Legionary Fortress 150 CE

The Legionary Fortress, looking north, in 150 CE.

The Legionary Fortress 150 CE

The Fortress was established around 71 CE and soon was surrounded by wooden walls, earth-banks and ditches. Between 107-108 CE the wooden fortress wall was replaced with a far more durable stone wall. It would have been around 4 metres *(13 feet)* high and surrounded the whole perimeter of the fortress. There were also four gatehouses which allowed entry into the fortress as well as a number of watchtowers. Most Roman fortresses followed a standard design of a rectangle with rounded corners. Other important fortresses in Roman Britain included: Chester, Lincoln and Caerleon *(South Wales)*. It is thought there **may** have been an annexe on the north-west side, which might have housed auxiliary forces. Most Roman Fortresses had an amphitheatre to entertain the troops. One has yet to be discovered, although in 2017 it was thought one **might** have been located in the area shown on the map.

Key

- Roman Walls
- Extent of Roman York
- 1) Tower
- 2) Gatehouse
- 3) Principia
- 4) Barracks
- 5) Fortress Bathhouse
- 6) Hospital
- 7) Granary
- 8) Workshop
- 9) Commander's quarters
- 10) Possible Amphitheatre
- 11) Possible Annexe

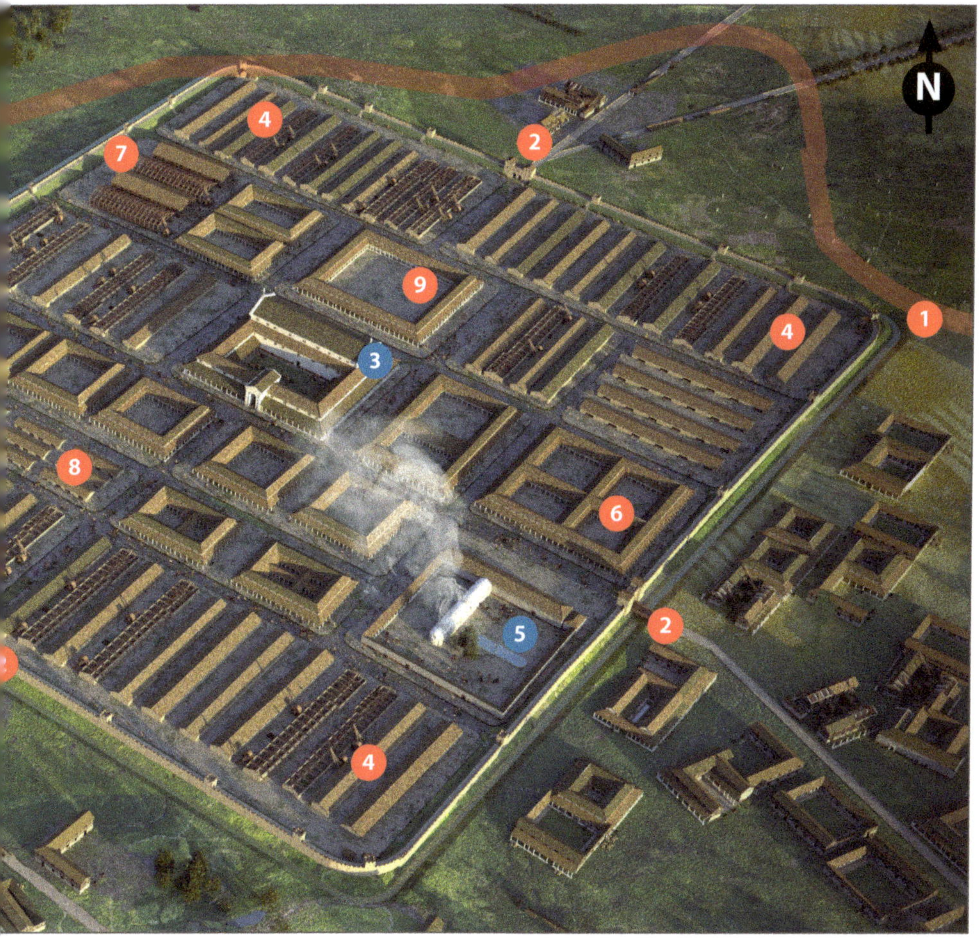

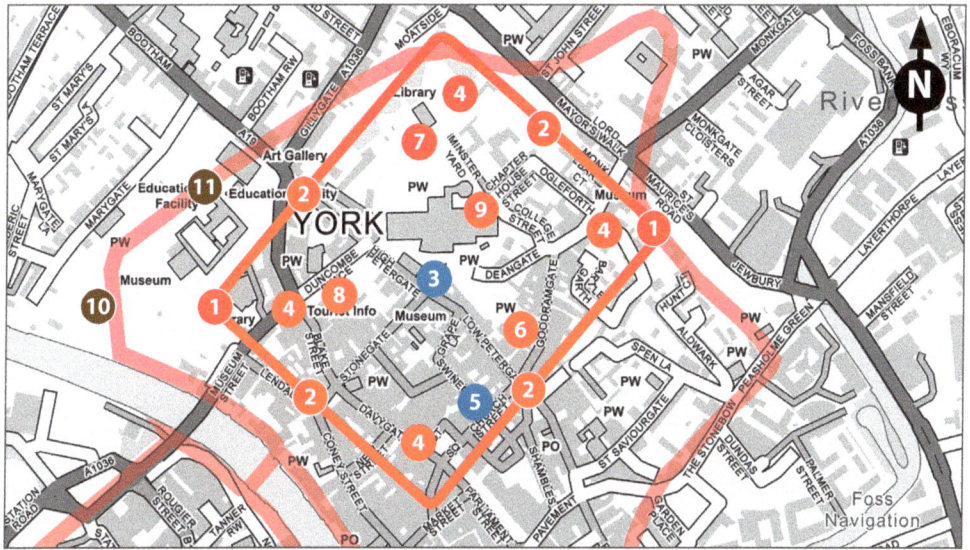

The Legionary Fortress, looking north, in 300 CE.

The Legionary Fortress 300 CE

Around 300 CE the defences along the west riverside were upgraded with towers and gatehouses featuring new designs: two corner towers *(including the Multangular Tower)*, six regular towers and a new gatehouse. These were all used to protect the fortress from possible attacks from the river. Around this time the Roman Empire was starting to face increasing problems internally and externally. Many Roman towns including York, London and Chichester began a programme of upgrades to their defences.

It is not known exactly how the fortress functioned around this time, but probably its role changed in many ways. By this time York was the capital of *Maxima Caesariensis*[1] and so it made sense to have a garrison protecting it.

1. Around 300 CE Roman Britain was probably split into four parts: Britannia Prima, Britannia Secunda, Maxima Caesariensis and Flavia Caesariensis.

Key

— Roman Walls
  Extent of Roman York
1 Multangular Tower
2 Bootham Bar
3 Senior Officers' Quarters
4 Stables
5 East Angle Tower
6 Gatehouse
7 Fortress Bathhouse
8 Riverside Towers
9 Possible Amphitheatre
10 Possible Annexe

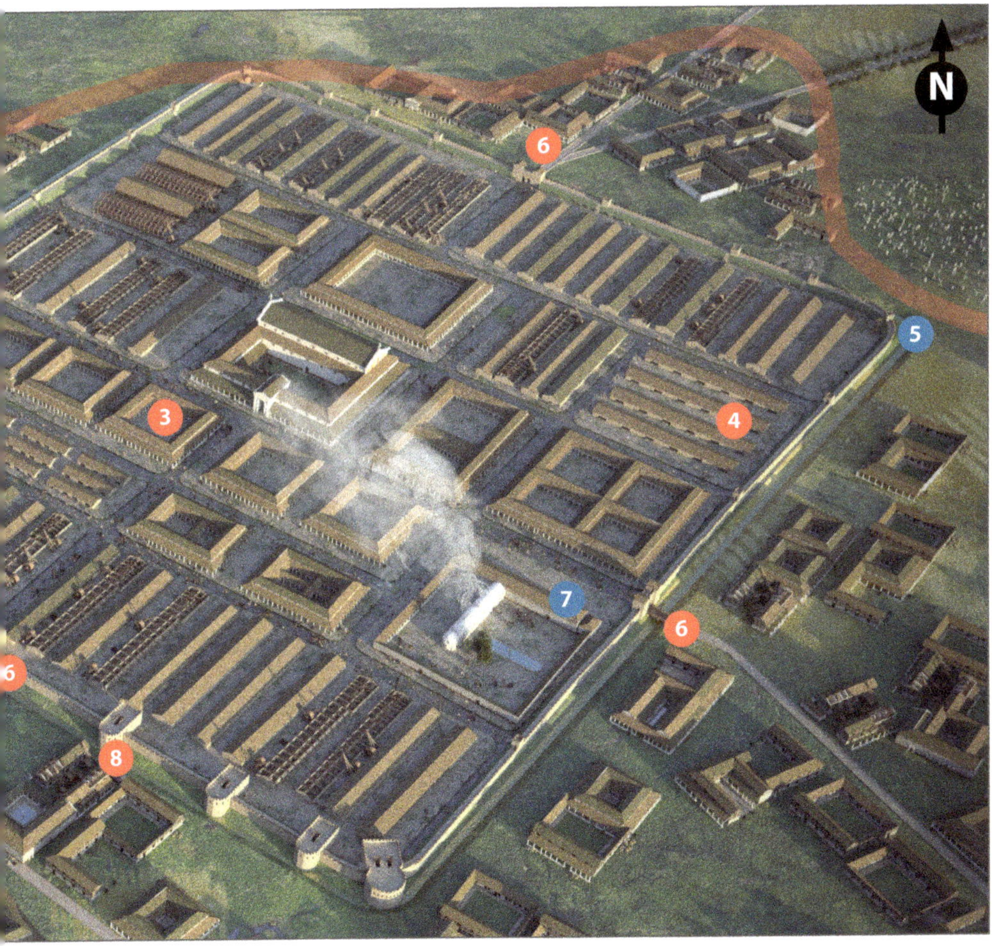

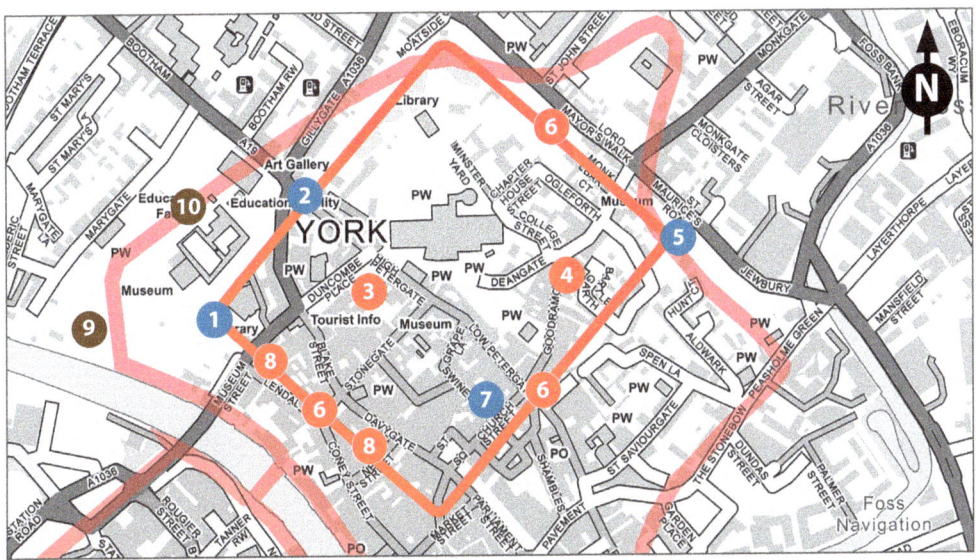

The Colonia, looking north, around 300 CE.

The Colonia

Around most fortresses in Roman Britain, including York, a small settlement called a *canaba* sprang up. It would have been full of locals hoping to offer the soldiers products and services. The *canaba* grew into a large area[1], with public buildings such as temples and a public bathhouse. Little is known about this area in detail. One area of debate is that the line of the medieval wall, south of the River Ouse, **might** originally have been Roman. This would follow the patterns of many large Roman settlements in Britain, but so far, there has been no evidence to support that theory. By 237 CE York had become a Colonia, which made it a settlement of great importance, along with Colchester, Lincoln and Gloucester. Part of the reason for Roman York's success may be due to its proximity to the River Ouse, which allowed ships from the Roman Empire to travel far inland to deliver their cargo.

1. Shown with a pale red line on the map.

Key

— Roman Walls
▢ Extent of Roman York
1. Fortress
2. Colonia
3. Temple of Serapis
4. Public Bathhouse
5. Cemetery
6. Roman Ship
7. Public Fountain
8. Fortress Bathhouse
9. Possible Amphitheatre
10. Possible Annexe
11. Possible Colonia Wall

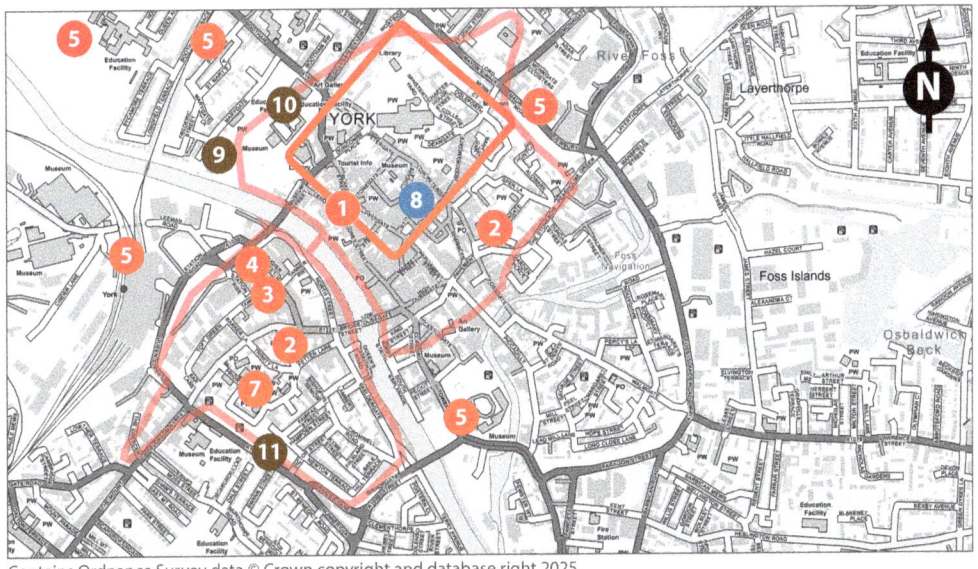

The site of the Multangular Tower, looking north, 300 CE.

The Multangular Tower

When the Roman Fortress was established around 71 CE, defences were soon built to protect the site, which included wooden towers on each corner. The defences were then rebuilt around 107 CE with stone walls, towers and gatehouses. Around 300 CE the defences were again upgraded along the riverside with a set of eight new towers *(including the Multangular Tower and a gatehouse)*. London also upgraded its river defences around 350 CE. The Multangular Tower featured a new advanced design with ten sides, rather than more typical four sides, and may have been around 10 metres *(33 feet)* high.

Another similar corner tower would have stood on the south-west corner of the fortress. *Ballistae*[1] may have been placed on all of the riverside towers to defend the fortress.

1. *Ballistae were huge crossbows that by the 4th century could fire stone balls or metal bolts.*

Key

- Roman Walls
- Extent of Roman York
- 1) Multangular Tower
- 2) Bootham Bar
- 3) Roman Legionaries
- 4) Barracks
- 5) Defensive ditch

4
4
N

MARYGATE
Education Facility
Education
2
cility
YORK
PW
PW
Museum
PW
DUNCOMBE PLACE
HIGH PETERGATE
PW
PW
DEANGATE
1
Library
4
Tourist Info
Museum
PW
BLAKE STREET
STONEGATE
GRAPE LA
SWINEGATE
LOW PE
MUSEUM STREET
LENDAL
PW
N

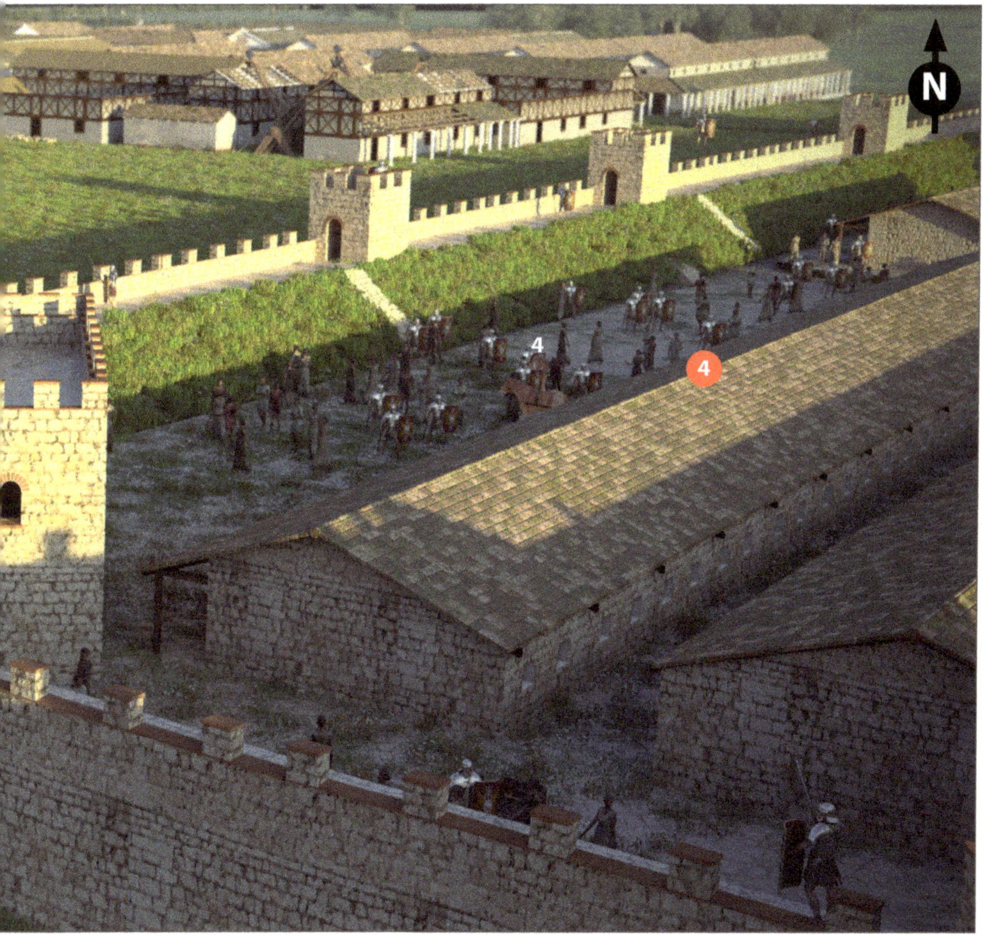

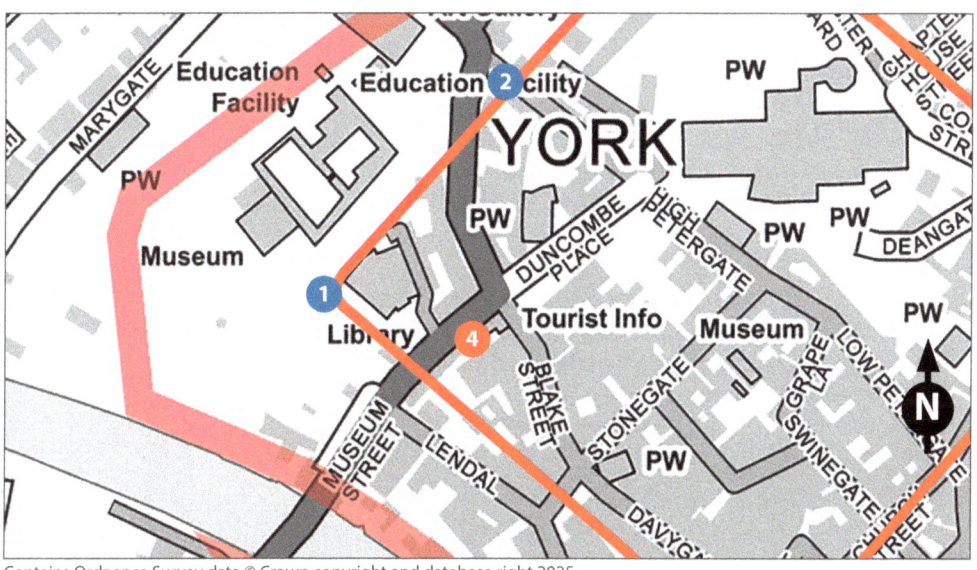

20. Bootham Bar

*The site of Bootham Bar, looking **east**, 300 CE.*

Bootham Bar

The fortress had four gatehouses, like most Roman fortresses. The *Porta Principalis Dextra (now known as Bootham Bar)* was the north-western gatehouse, leading directly to the *Principia (legionary headquarters)* along the *Via Principalis (present day Petergate)*. From this side of the fortress the legions would have marched north to *Isurium Brigantum (Aldborough),* Hadrian's Wall and beyond. *Porta Principalis Dextra* roughly translates as *main right gate*, and would have had a central arch for wheeled traffic, and narrower arches at the sides for people on foot. Above the gatehouse centurions, legionaries and auxiliaries would have defended the fortress, using round stones and javelins.

After the Romans
The gatehouse was still in use by the 7th century and its current name dates from the 12th century. The name seems to mean **bar** *(gate) near the* **booth** *(market booth).*

Key
- Roman Walls
- Extent of Roman York
- **1** Bootham Bar
- **2** Multangular Tower
- **3** Barracks
- **4** Defensive ditch
- **5** Granaries

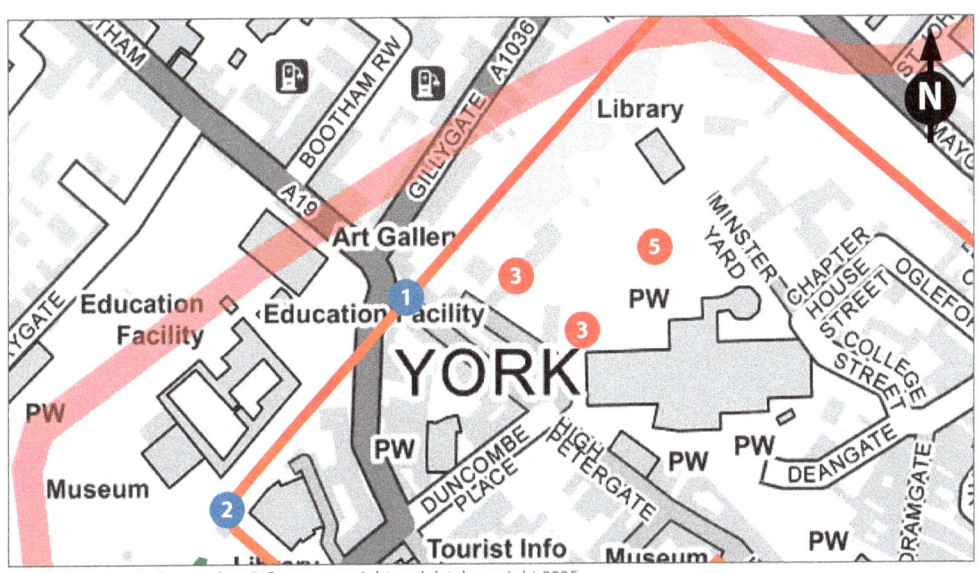

22. The Fortress Bathhouse

A speculative view of the Fortress Bathhouse, looking north, 300 CE.

The Fortress Bathhouse

On the south-west side of the fortress was a large bathhouse, which would have had a furnace to heat the *Caldarium (hot room)* and the *Tepidarium (warm room)*. There was also a *Frigidarium (cold room)*, and a large *Palaestra (exercise area)*. The soldiers would have bathed and socialised, in some ways like in our present day swimming pools. The Romans did not have soap products, so instead used oil and scraped the oil off with a curved implement called a strigil. The bathhouse may have had many other facilities such as an *Apodyterium (heated changing rooms)* and possibly a library. It might have been supplied with water from an aqueduct, but none has yet been found. Parts of the bathhouse can still be seen today in a small pub on Sampson Square *(marked with the yellow box 'C')*. Another public bathhouse was uncovered in 1839 on the site of the old railway station, but its exact design is unknown.

Key

- ▬ *Roman Walls*
- ▢ *Extent of Roman York*
- **1** *Fortress Bathhouse*
- **2** *Hot room*
- **3** *Warm room*
- **4** *Cold room*
- **5** *Exercise area*
- **6** *Public Bathhouse*
- **7** *Principia*

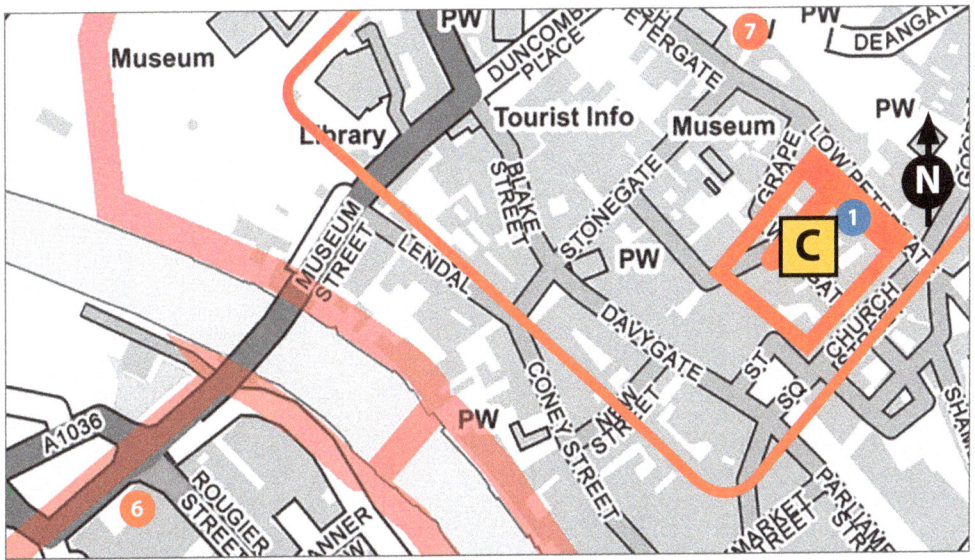

The site of the Principia, looking north, 300 CE.

The Principia

The *Principia* was the centre of the fortress where the Legionary standards[1] would be kept along with the soldiers' pay. It also acted as the administrative hub of the fortress, such as the logistics needed to keep the fortress maintained and everyone fed. Most Roman fortresses had two main roads, the *Via Principalis* (loosely translated as the 'way to the Principia') and the *Via Praetoria* (loosely translated as 'the way to the Praetorium'). The *Legatus Legionis* (a rough equivalent of a general) typically occupied the *Praetorium* (shown on the main image, just behind the Principia[2]). Here matters such as how the army would be deployed were discussed.

1. Standards were symbols carried into battle on tall poles, which partly represented the legion and the power of Rome.
2. York Minster is built on the site of the Principia and has the Undercroft Museum showing what the fortress looked like (The yellow square on the map).

Key

— Roman Walls
 Extent of Roman York
1. Basilica[3]
2. Barracks
3. Fortress Tower
4. Granaries
5. Praetorium
6. Via Principalis
7. Via Praetoria

3. One column from the Basilica can be seen on the south side of York Minster.

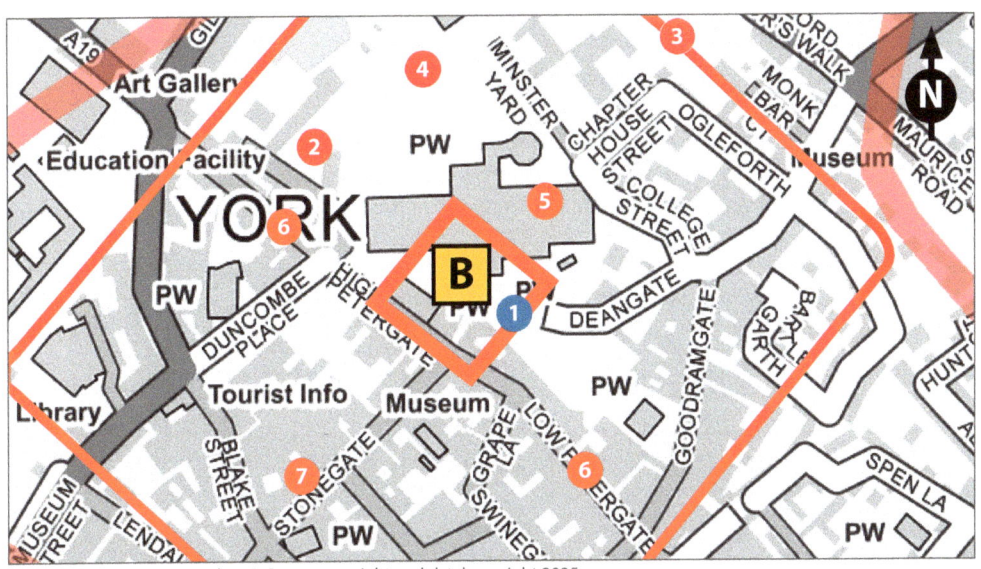

Possible site of the Barracks, looking north, 300 CE.

The Barracks

The soldiers based at York all needed accommodation which was called a *Praetentura (Barrack)*. A barrack housed a Legionary *century (made up of eighty Legionaries and a Centurion)*. Each barrack was probably split into two sections, one for commanding officers such as the Centurion and one for the eighty Legionaries. The Centurion would have had space appropriate to his rank, including an office to keep each *century* running properly. This involved logistics and discipline. There was far less space for the Legionaries who were split into groups of eight, each with two rooms, one for them and one for their equipment. Spare rooms were used to accommodate new recruits or other soldiers. Extra rooms were typically used to house replacement soldiers or clerks assigned to the legion.
Sometimes soldiers and their horses lived in the same barracks, such as the barracks built at Hadrian's Wall.

Key

- Roman Walls
- Extent of Roman York
- ① Barracks
- ② Defensive ditch
- ③ Fortress Wall
- ④ Multangular Tower
- ⑤ Riverside Tower
- ⑥ Gatehouse

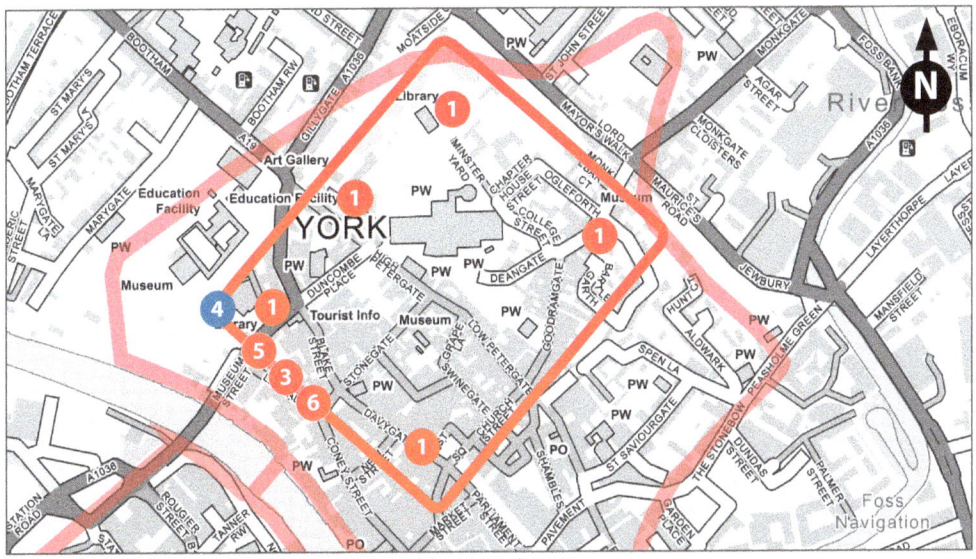

A view of the Granaries, looking north, 300 CE.

The Granaries

Supplying all the soldiers with food would have been a major operation. Wheat grain was one of the main food sources for the soldiers, stored *(along with many other types of food)* in purpose-built structures such as the *Horrea (granaries)* shown in the main image. The granaries would have built on raised feet to stop vermin such as rats eating the stored food. The Romans had a wide range of food from all across the Roman Empire, although meat would have been a luxury. Common foods included: olive oil, vegetables, herbs, fish sauces and coarse-grain breads. When the soldiers were out on patrol they would have had rations of wheat to make *Panis militaris (army bread)* and other basic foods.
If the Fortress at York was similar to the one at Caerleon in Wales, it may have had small ovens spread around the walls to feed the soldiers. These were either exterior ovens or ovens located inside small cook-houses.

Key

— *Roman Walls*
Extent of Roman York
1. *Granary*
2. *Fortress Wall*
3. *Corner Tower*

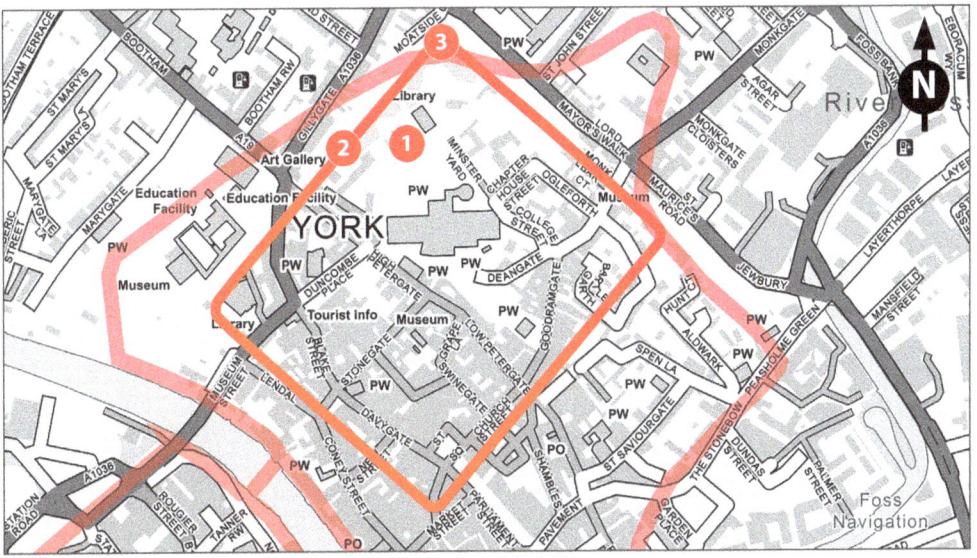

A view showing typical weapons and equipment used by the Ninth Legion.

The Ninth Legion

The *Legio IX Hispana (Ninth Spanish Legion)*, which established the fortress at York, was one of the original four legions which invaded Britain in 43 CE. After the invasion they fought native tribes in the west and built a fortress in Lincoln in 50 CE. The Ninth Legion was to suffer devastating losses trying to relieve Roman forces fighting *Boudica*[1] in Colchester in 60-61 CE. By 71 CE the Ninth Legion had established York after defeating the local *Brigantes*, but were to just escape destruction from a night attack by forces in *Caledonia (present day Scotland)*. What happened to the Ninth Legion after that has become something of a mystery, the last known record of them was at York.

Some think they were wiped out after 108 CE in Caledonia, while others believe it happened in Judea *(present day Palestine/Israel)* or Armenia.

1. Boudica and 120,000 warriors burnt Colchester to the ground.

Key

1. *Pilum (Javelin)*[2]
2. *Scutum (Shield)*
3. *Focale (Scarf)*
4. *Gladius (Sword)*
5. *Galea (Helmet)*
6. *Lorica Segmentata (Body Armour)*
7. *Tunica (Tunic)*
8. *Caligae (Sandals)*

2. The Yorkshire Museum has many artefacts from the Ninth Legion.

A possible route used by the Ninth Legion from 43 CE to 71 CE

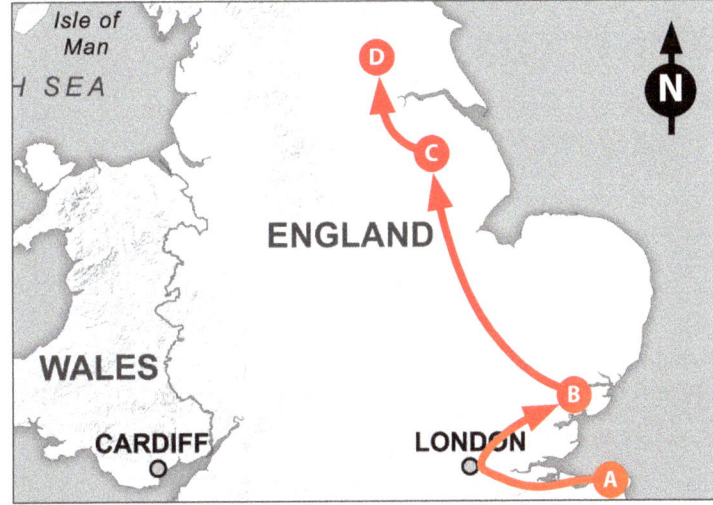

- A Richborough
- B Colchester
- C Lincoln
- D York

32. Roman York today

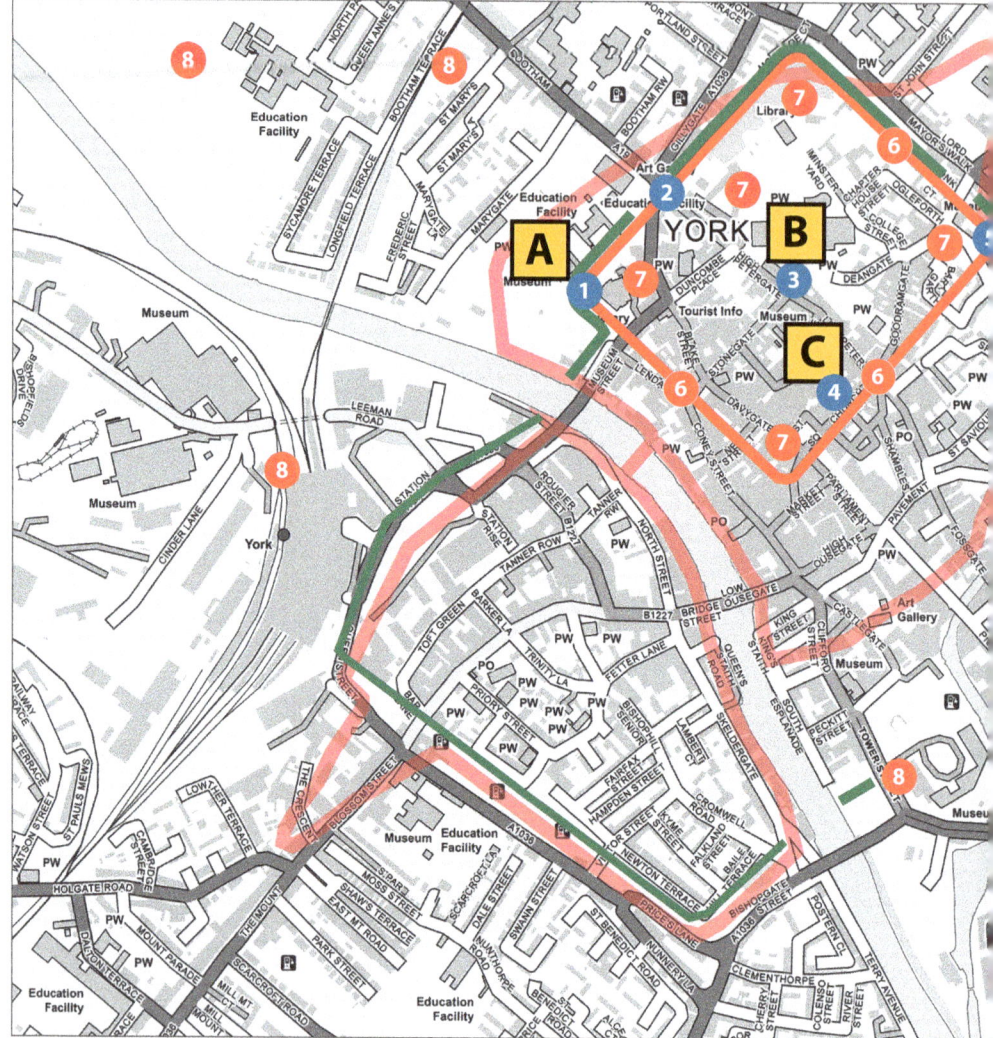

Roman York today

While York is possibly best known for its Viking heritage, the city has extensive Roman sites and artefacts.
It can be difficult to interpret what is Roman and what is post-Roman, especially with the city walls. Most of the city walls visible today date from after the Roman period.
The sites shown on this map are also explored in more detail in the main part of this book, as well as showing where the main museums in York are that feature Roman artefacts.
Some sites highlighted in this book are speculative, see inside for details.

Key

① *Roman site, with visible remains*

② *Roman site, with no visible remains*

— *Roman wall, no visible remains*

Extent of Roman York

Ⓐ *Museum, which has visible Roman artefacts/remains*

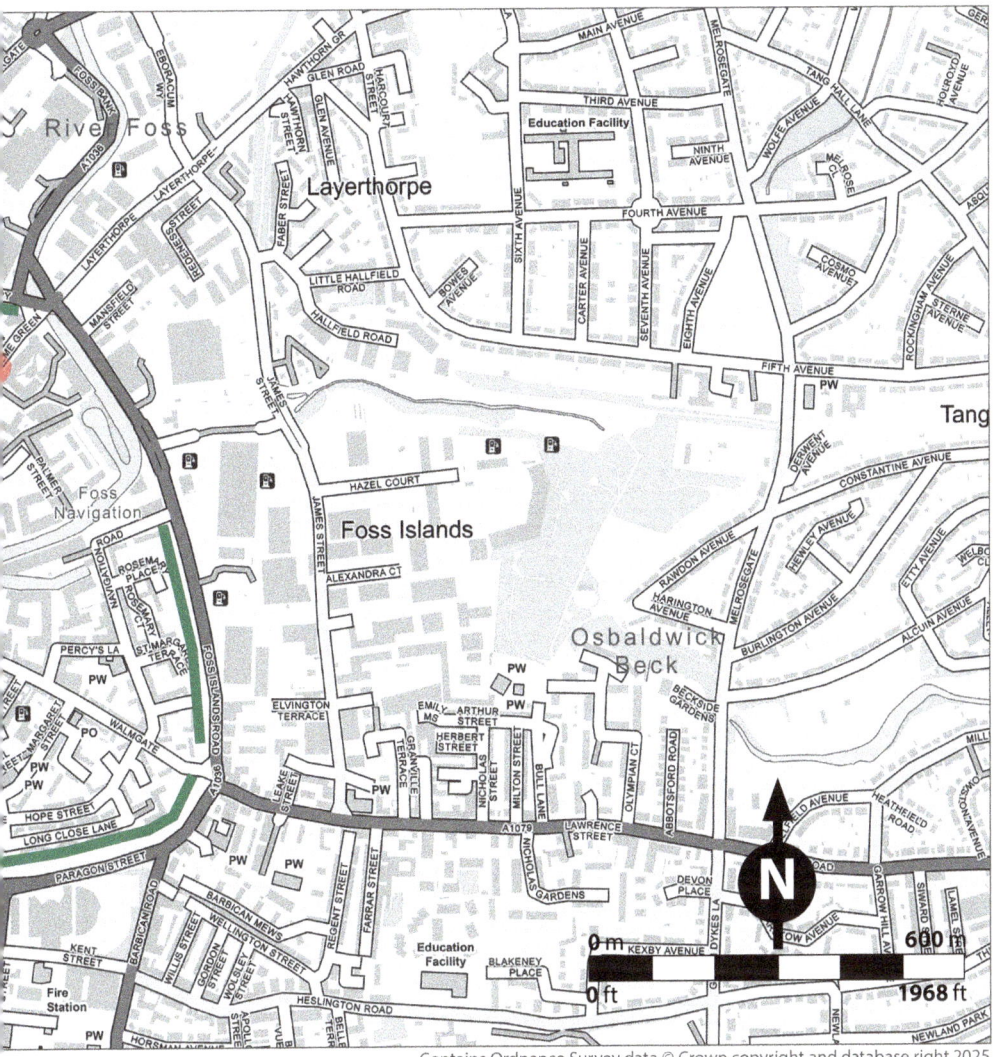

Post-Roman wall, with visible remains
1. Multangular Tower (p. 18)
2. Bootham Bar (p. 20)
3. Principia (p. 24)
4. Fortress Bathhouse (p. 22)
5. East Angle Tower (p. 14)
6. Gatehouse (p. 14)
— Roman Fortress (p.12/14)
7. Barracks (p. 26)
8. Cemetery (p. 8)

A. The Yorkshire Museum
B. Undercroft Museum, York Minster
C. Roman Bath Museum

First published June 2023
ISBN 978-1-7391254-2-4 *(Paperback)*
Third Edition

Designed and published by JC3DVIS
www.jc3dvis.co.uk
Book design © 2024 Joseph Chittenden

All the images in this guide were produced by JC3DVIS.
Contains Ordnance Survey data © Crown copyright and database right 2024

The moral right of the copyright holder has been asserted.

All rights reserved. No part of this publication may be reproduced, distributed or transmitted in any form or by any means, including photocopying, recording, or other electronic or mechanical methods, without the prior written permission of the publisher.

With special thanks to:
Jane Chittenden *(Research, writing and proofreading)*
Valerie Graves

Legal disclaimer
Neither the author nor the publisher shall be held liable or responsible to any person or entity with respect to any loss or incidental or consequential damages caused, or alleged to have been caused, directly or indirectly, by the information contained herein.

Bibliography and sources

- Chrystal. P and Drake. I: *The making of Roman York*
- Goldsworthy. A: *The Complete Roman Army*
- *https://her.york.gov.uk/Monument/MYO1075 (Multangular Tower)*
- *https://her.york.gov.uk/Monument/MYO2015 (Legionary Fortress)*
- *https://her.york.gov.uk/Monument/MYO3630 (Possible fort annexe)*
- *https://her.york.gov.uk/Monument/MYO4171(Possible Roman bridge)*
- *https://her.york.gov.uk/Monument/MYO4173 (2nd Roman Bathhouse)*
- *https://her.york.gov.uk/Monument/MYO4226 (Bootham Bar)*
- Lewis. M: *Migration and Diversity in Roman Britain: A Multidisciplinary Approach to the Identification of Immigrants in Roman York, England (accessed online)*
- McComish. J et al *(York Archaeological Trust): Roman Burials at16-22 Coppergate, York (accessed online)*
- Ordnance Survey/York Archaeological Trust: *Roman and Anglian York*
- Ottaway. P *(York Archaeological Trust): Archaeology in the Environs of Roman York (accessed online)*
- *Temple to Serapis in Roman York - Yorkshire Museum (Youtube)*

www.ingramcontent.com/pod-product-compliance
Lightning Source LLC
Chambersburg PA
CBHW042123100526
44587CB00025B/4159